Frau Perchta: The Christmas Belly-Slitter
A Concise History of the Legend
By Edmund Breckin

'I do nothing to the pious, the evil I will plague'

'Silence, or the wild Berta is coming!'

Contents

Introduction

The festive season, behind the joy, Christmas spirit, and tender emotions towards friends and family, has always traditionally had a relationship with ghost stories and festive ghouls. Think of Charles Dickens *A Christmas Carol* or the festive horror stories of MR James told by a crackling fire. Maybe it is the chill of a winter's eve or the long dark evenings but Christmas has always been a superb time to share in tales of ghostly apparitions, and fearsome creatures. As Jerome K Jerome aptly introduced a Victorian anthology of Christmas ghostly tales 'whenever five or six English speaking people meet round a fire on Christmas eve, they start telling each other ghost stories. Nothing satisfies us on Christmas Eve but to hear each other tell authentic anecdotes about spectres'. But what of the tales which are not stories created by an author? What about the legends of spectres who haunt Christmas? We all know Father Christmas and his naughty or nice list; be good and expect to receive a gift, be naughty and Santa may leave just a lump of coal, or maybe nothing at all! However Santa isn't the only festive spirit who frequents the Festive season, and unlike Santa, this other spirit dishes out a far more terrifying punishment for those on her naughty list. This book will cover the history of the Christmas Belly-Slitter, Frau Perchta, so get comfortable by the fire and rekindle some of that ghostly Christmas spirit.

Who was, or who is, Frau Perchta? The legend so predominant through Germanic and Austrian folklore who has had somewhat a rekindling in contemporary times with ever more exuberant celebrations during the Christmas period? She is regularly conflated with the character Krampus, whom will shall touch on shortly, either as an amalgamation of their separate identities or as his partner in crime or counterpart; but it is really not that simple. The two characters do share traits, the beastly evil depictions, but Frau Perchta could just as easily be associated with Father Christmas. She shares the same magical gift-giver status, she is at large during the 12 days of Christmas, she is left food for her nocturnal visits, rewards those who abide by her preordained rules, and looks askance on those who fail to do so. Pinpointing her legend is difficult as it takes on so many variations from so many locations which makes succinctly describing her difficult but she is nowadays notoriously known as the evil Perchta. Her infamous method for punishing adults and children for their misbehaviour maybe precedes any lay person's knowledge of her legend. For Perchta, her sinister way of punishing the slovenly was to rip open their stomachs whilst they slept, remove their entrails and intestines before stuffing them with refuse and dirt, sewing them back up again and leaving them to be discovered the next morning by family who perceive the poor person has merely died peacefully in the night. This is aptly why she is often referred to as the festive belly-slitter.

Perchta however was far more than a monstrous Christmas spectre haunting those who behaved badly; she is regularly described in this manner nowadays, tearing asunder, eating and disembowelling those who disobey her but she was much more than this interpretation. Not only does she have a dual nature and a side to her legend which is both kind yet violent, haggard yet beautiful, old but young, she also rewarded those who had behaved all year round with silver coins. But Perchta's power went beyond the festive behavioural social control which we associate with Santa and being naughty or nice; to many she was all powerful, more akin to a god or deity than merely a legend. She had strong links to nature, living in the mountains and lakes, and she had power of the snow and seasons, both bringing on the beginning and end of winter. Her origins are murky, without any records to say where and when the legend precisely began but it appears that she derived from extractions of differing Germanic goddesses who were part of Germanic paganism in the Alpine region. This is mainly extrapolated from her name, the word deriving from Old High German language meaning 'bright' or 'shining one' and its origin suggesting an old indigenous history. Her association with Christmas appears to stem from this interpretation of her name,

Perchtentag or 'bright day' has become the Epiphany which now in the legend in her sacred day for all to respect her wishes or feel the consequences. As we will discover later her fall from pagan goddess powerful over nature and winter may have withered to its current level as Christmas witch as Christianity enveloped pagan traditions.

This book will explore the legend of Frau Perchta, the witch who haunts the misbehaving during Christmas. Along with her entourage of ghosts and dead children, she visits homes during the twelve days between Christmas and Epiphany. Her rewards are generous and she can grant good luck for a full upcoming year, but she also punishes the lazy, the dishonest, greedy, and curious. She has demands regarding what you can and cannot eat on her day and she has a special interest in spinning. She expected everyone to participate in her festive celebrations, so anyone who shirked their responsibilities or failed to celebrate with their neighbours could meet their grisly fate by her jagged knife. Adults and children, masters and servants, rich and poor, everyone was vulnerable to her punishments which were as varied and creative as they needed to be; belly slitting, boiling alive, glass scraping your tongue, she was monstrous when she needed to be. Where do these customs come from? Why the belly-slitting? Why did she become so associated with spinning? And Christmas? Why is her effort to enforce obedience more the stick than the carrot when Father Christmas became almost her opposite? This book will try and answer some of these questions by examining her history, and her legend, her traits, and how she is currently portrayed in contemporary Festive traditions. This is the legend of Frau Perchta, the Christmas belly-slitter.

Ghoulish festive relations

Frau Perchta is not the only Christmas entity who haunts those who have misbehaved, she has a number of monstrous cousins, some of which she is mistakenly associated but all are out to seek punishment for the wicked at Christmas. The creature Perchta is most closely related is probably the most infamous of the monsters of Christmas; Krampus. Perchta is often depicted in appearance resembling Krampus closely, the horns, hooves, fur, and beast like body is probably why she is often referred to as the partner of Krampus. She is regularly said to accompany Krampus in his hunts for naughty children in the advent of Christmas. They also have similarities in their followers of goblins and ghouls, and it is possible this is why their imagery sometimes becomes convoluted and mixed. Whilst similar to Krampus, they are different entities with different backgrounds but their legends sometimes are told to include each other so the distinction sometimes becomes rather fuzzy. As she sometimes borrows from other legends, it seems appropriate to outline some of her evil Christmas cousins before delving deeper into her legend.

KRAMPUS

The horned, hoofed, furry beast that was said to accompany Santa on his rounds, sometimes described as anti-Santa or even his evil twin, Krampus is the best known of evil Christmas creatures. Krampus is closely linked to Father Christmas, often where Santa serves to reward the good, Krampus was seen as the punisher of the bad, hence why they are so interlinked in Christmas folklore. Despite many versions of the Krampus legend believing that he accompanied Saint Nicholas as he visited the world's children, he actually has his own day. Krampus Night is celebrated on December 5th in many parts of Europe, particularly Austria. In fact, much like the beast they celebrate, many public festivals have been curtailed in recent years due to the violent behaviour of some of the Krampus dressed festival goers. Krampus inflicts punishment much like Perchta but his modus operandi is to beat any misbehaving children with a cluster of sticks. If this did not suffice, sometimes a particularly naughty child would be taken away in Krampus's basket, never to be seen again.

The name comes from the old German word for claw *Krampen* (or Kralle, in modern German), and his existence is as old as Perchtas, stretching back to medieval Europe. His beast-like demeanour was an effective threat to badly behaved children, the horned anthropomorphic creature with claws was a convenient way to scare children into good behaviour once the threat of not receiving a gift from Saint Nicholas had been exhausted. Krampus has had a renaissance in recent years and even crossed over to Western movie and television, so it appears Saint Nicholas' twin will continue to frighten children over Christmas.

JÓLAKÖTTURINN

The Icelandic Yule Cat, Jolakotturinn, is the next festive monster on Perchta's family tree. Whilst the regional and appearance differences are drastically removed from Perchta, the Christmas Cat took relish in punishing the lazy. The character is born from an Icelandic tradition in which children that have finished all their work and behaved well would receive new clothes at Christmas, and those who did not would have no new clothes and have another year using their old clothes. Much like the traditional reward and punishment approach of all our Christmas folklores, sometimes this reward or nothing approach was no sufficient to encourage lazy children to work hard, so the Yule Cat was created. Jólakötturinn is not a nice cat, and in fact is happy to eat any children who have been lazy the past year and he has an ingenious way to know who has been naughty and who has been nice. If the Yule Cat sees any children without new items of clothing, he would know they had been lazy that year and not completed all their chores and therefore they were ready to be eaten at Christmas. Another method at social control where the stick was needed in addition to the carrot, Jólakötturinn shares Perchta's dislike for anyone deemed lazy.

BELSNICKEL

Belsnickel is a character that some readers may have heard of mainly due to the fact his legend has crossed from Europe over to the United States. Originated in German folklore, the name is a portmanteau of the German word for walloping or beating, *Belzen*, combined with the nickel which comes from Saint Nicholas's name. Again Belsnickel has a strong relationship with Father Christmas, leaving St Nicholas to dole out the rewards for good behaviour and Belsnickel could in turn dole out the punishments to misbehaving children at Christmas. He travelled to the states with Dutch emigrants and continues in traditional folklore, particularly in Pennsylvania due to its Dutch history. He is said to be very shabbily dressed with a pointy little beard, and ragged in appearance. He also had the potential to give out rewards as was supposed to carry candy as well as a switch which could scare children through its noise. The noise supposedly allowed children a warning to know there was still time for them to mend their ways before Christmas came around. Both Knecht Ruprecht and Ru Klaas are similar

German folklore characters who dish out similar beatings as Belsnickel and have strong links with Father Christmas.

HANS TRAPP

In the Alsace and Lorraine region of France, Hans Trapp is a similar figure to Belsnikel, also revelling in dealing out punishments to misbehaving children. Hans Trapp however has a more sinister appearance. The legend says that Hans Trapp was actually a real person who was horrible in life, evil to the core, rich, greedy, and similarly unpleasant to children. An apparent Satanist, Hans Trapp was exiled from his home town by the Catholic Church and went to live in the forests away from civilisation. As evil as before but now in isolation, Hans Trapp began to disguise himself as a scarecrow, covering in straw, protruding from his clothes. He had captured a child using his disguise and was taking the child back to his forest lair when he was hit by lightning. The lightening killed Hans Trapp and was according to legend, sent as a punishment from God for all the evil he had done. Whether this back story is true or not, Hans

Trapp is now used in the same vain as the other Christmas monsters, as a way to threaten misbehaving children. If they do still misbehave, they can expect to have a visit from Hans Trapp, still in his scarecrow clothes at Christmas, scaring them rigid into good behaviour.

PÈRE FOUETTARD

Another French Christmas ghoul arose from Saint Nicholas's own legend. Pere Fouettard, whose name translates as 'Father Whipper' is another anti-Santa, dealing in punishments of the naughty at Christmas. However his origins draw from Santa's own backstory. Pere Fouettard was an evil butcher who used his butchery skills to serve his own desires for children to eat. Three children one day had been playing until the sun had gone down, not usually staying out so long; they were lost, tired, and hungry. The saw the light coming from the butcher's shop and went inside looking for shelter; Pere Fouettard obliged happily. He killed the three children before cutting them into meat size portions and salting the meat, he left the pieces of salted meat in his salting tub for him to enjoy later. After time had passed, Bishop Saint Nicholas appeared at the Butcher's shop and demanded that the evil Pere show him his salting tub; there lay the remains of the children. Saint Nicholas called upon God and told the children to rise up, and the children were resurrected and went home to their loving families. The children were saved by Father Christmas himself, and from there he became the patron saint of children and his legend began. Pere Fouettard's legend begins there, Saint Nicholas taking the evil butcher captive as his servant and his job for ever more is to punish children who misbehave on Saint Nicholas Day.

Perchta shares traits with many of the festive monsters who haunt children in different countries across the world. Her appearance is often likened to Krampus, whereas the Italian Christmas witch *La Befana* who was said to be very ugly and scary is also an appearance which Perchta sometimes shares depending on the region. All the above Christmas ghouls share Perchta's proclivity for punishment of the wicked, lazy, or misbehaving, but Perchta also had the ability to reward those whom she deemed as well behaved. Whilst she is known for her affiliation to Christmas, she is less reliant and related to Santa Claus than many of the anti-Santa creatures listed previously. This is why her legend needs telling in full, as she is more than the run of the mill anti-Christmas but still with the sinister streak of evil whenever she deems it appropriate.

Legend

Attempting to present a concise summary of the legend and Frau Perchta is a difficult task to undertake. So influential was Perchta's legend spanning such a large part of Europe that different regions and even different villages and towns have their own interpretations; you could be told the Perchta legend by two different individuals and reach the conclusion they were talking of different creatures, with Christmas the only link. Similarly so, her durability through the age's means that the contexts to her legend and purpose have been amended, from preoccupations with fast and feast, through spinning, to punishing the slovenly, she alters to punish those deemed punishable during a certain era's context. Whilst we will discuss these different idiosyncrasies of her legend as we go on, looking at her different appearances and food likes and dislikes, this section will try and present an overall depiction of the legend. Difficult it may be but there are a number of traits of the legend which appear with more consistency than others and therefore a good place with giving the legend some structure. As I have mentioned, some aspects are so varied such as her appearance that these will command their own section later, but here is the outline of the Perchta legend, perfect for telling to any wayward children you may know to scare them straight before Christmas.

A combination of interpretations leaves us with the image of a deity born of the wild and with strong relationship to nature, particularly winter and snowfall. She has a dual nature, both able to reward the well behaved and punish the wicked, and she shows a concern with the moral education of the young and those involved with the process of spinning flax. She was often accompanied by followers, beings which can be described between mortal and immortal, sometimes ghosts of children, animals, or just ghouls and mischief makers, generally always in a malicious frenzy, and not usually seen, more heard from the cacophony they make riding through the mountains and villages. Perchta and her band of ghosts roamed the countryside during midwinter, and sought to enter the homes she passed between the twelve days of Christmas, from Christmas Day through to Epiphany, Twelfth Night is considered her festival night so she is even more active on the day of the feast of the Three Kings. When entering each house her dual nature would shine through, she would know who had worked well and hard through the year and they would be rewarded with a small silver coin which they might find the next day in a shoe. For the less fortunate, who Perchta felt had been lazy the past year, they would have their bellies sliced open whilst they slept, the insides removed before they were stuffed with dirt, dust, pebbles, straw, or refuge. This reward or punishment was dealt out to any spinners depending on whether they had spun their allotted portion for the year, and whether they had spun on any prohibited days, such as Twelfth Night.

There are ways to help avoid her wrath, potent herbs can be burned or hung around the home which prevent her from bring bad luck to the home, and this is generally the herb St John 's wort. At Christmas and on Epiphany, leaving certain foods out for Perchta will keep her happy and appeased; this could be a spoonful of every dish from the Yuletide feast, left outside on a gate, the path, sometimes on the roof as an offering. Her standing ranges from someone from the ghouls or fairy realm, akin to a guardian spirit, whereas others see her as a deity, a pagan goddess with power over winter.

Her punishments are varied and we will cover some of these in more detail when we look at the most popular stories about Perchta, but beyond belly slitting she had other powers of punishment. She often punished the inquisitive or derisive with a curse of a year of blindness; she would boil spinners alive if they spun on prohibited days; she could grant a year's bad luck to an individual or a full village; she could tread on children, crushing them to death; but her most memorable and justifiably most feared was her penchant for using a sickle/knife/scissors to slitting open and gutting her victims. Perhaps the most dastardly of this crime was that she would then sew the victim back closed with a needle made of iron, so when whoever discovered your corpse the next morning would see no evidence of foul play and assume you had died a peaceful death in the night. She was however not all punishment, and for those who worked hard and were deemed worthy, she would leave silver coins in the house which they would discover the next morning; blessings to those when she is offered food and good fortune; and her pleasure at seeing a neat and tidy home would mean a payment of gold to the household. She is better known for her acts of cruelty, but Perchta could be equally kind if she deemed the individual worthy of her rewards. Sometimes she can be the embodiment of goodness and charity, but sometimes she can be full of malice and hatred, her dual identity mean that people mingled feelings of fear and trepidation with awe and longing because of her omniscient powers.

Perchta has an affinity with children, and she is often surrounded by them when she makes her visits during the twelve days of Christmas. Many of these children are the spirits, neither dead nor undead, of children who died before they could be blessed by baptismal water. The smallest child is often at the rear of her cohort of children, burdened with a pitcher it carries full of the tears of mothers of the children but this child can be saved by any human who sees it and gives it a name. Sometimes these children take on the form of a canine as they have transformed and Perchta also has a strong connection to animals and nature. Dogs are often seen when children are not and can be heard following her carriage barking and howling long before her wild hunt begins. She also has an association with goats and is said she has the ability to transform into a goat whenever she wishes. The owl is her own personal sacred animal and is seen as her personal messenger, passing on information about who has been good and who has been bad; due to this, the presence of owls is seen as an omen of danger or death. As she is often referred to as 'Wild' due to her kinship with nature, she is seen as belonging to the forest and mountains and has no set dwelling place. Sometimes she is depicted as having a cave but generally she is seen as being at one with groves and glens, the snow fall is controlled by her and she is one with the season of winter.

As we referred to earlier, Perchta is often depicted in the group of followers behind Krampus; this confusion arises from the fact that both Krampus and Perchta have their own train of ghouls and ghosts who join them on their hunts and travels. Perchta's legend originates in the legend of the 'Wild Hunt' which is synonymous with a number of folklore legends and their own hunts. The Wild Hunt is comprised of ghouls, goblins, fairies, and demons running around causing mischief and enjoying their night of flamboyant evilness. Seeing this hunt in action is thought to be an omen for great misfortune or that the whole village may be in for a bad year. As mentioned, the Wild Hunt is a common legend in the Alpine region of Europe and associated with numerous characters, but in some renditions, Perchta is said to lead the hunt. The Hunt is characterised by a frenzy of noises, bells, screams, animals howling, whips cracking, the noises hurrying down the mountains in a din, generally with Perchta heading the orgiastic train. Apart from seeing the Hunt being bad luck, being in its path can be fatal, either from being crushed by the procession or killed by one of the wicked creatures within the hunt. The clamour of beasts and noises in procession has been portrayed in festival celebrations and rituals since medieval times and we will discuss this later; its replication in festive celebrations remains to this day. Perchta's procession varies depending on legend; she was always said to be followed by the ghosts of unbaptized children who had died and this is the most common depiction of her cohort of followers. This however may have been altered as Christianity began to exert influence upon her legend and sought to highlight the importance of baptism. Previous to this her orgiastic train was more akin to the frenzy of ghouls and hobgoblins travelling through the night in a hunt of wickedness. Less frequently, her procession included a visual demonstration of her evisceration skills, her victims, young and old, trailing behind her with their entrails falling behind them.

The 'Wild Hunt' whilst popular in many regions and with other goddesses leading the winter hunt may seem like it has been simply added to the Perchta legend, it did actually have real life consequences during the height of its popularity. So fervent was belief in the Wild Hunt that imitations did occur of followers running in frenzied processions through village streets. A Bavarian manuscript from the 15th century describes how a woman believed to be under the leadership of Perchta ran frenzied through a village approaching houses during the Christmas season. Evidence taken from witch trials show that some people confessed to being part of the wild host trains and servants of Frau Perchta. This does not constitute evidence for Perchta or her wild hunt but it demonstrates how ingrained the beliefs in her legend were during this period. The stories of her power to grant rewards and dish out punishment travelled across the region, and soon families both rich and poor were telling tales of Frau Perchta and her legend, and with it her proclivity for disembowelling the wicked.

Stories

As with any legend, it is the stories which are passed on by a warm crackling fire, or by our parents when tucked up in bed which become the way the legend transcends through generations and across geographical boundaries. Below are a number of the Frau Perchta stories which appear with the most frequency, albeit with variations, but the basic premise remains the same. The structure of each of these stories is found across Germany and Austria but changes which are appropriate to regions Perchta legend may be added to the story. These stories were collected by Richard Wolfram in the mid twentieth century by speaking to locals about the story of Perchta and her festive punishments.

The farmhand

This story has many similarities to the stories of Santa Claus and of children not sneaking down to catch a glimpse of St Nicholas as he delivers his presents, however this has a Perchta style twist to the story. As Twelfth Night approached and the snow covered the hills, a farmer's wife and her helpers from her household were preparing the farm for the arrival of Perchta and her followers. When the room and home had been prepared, an inquisitive farmhand decided that he wanted a glimpse of Perchta when she arrived so he snuck into the great stove in the room which was to be Perchta's. Pressing his eye against a small hole in the door of the stove he could see into the room without anyone even knowing he was there! When Perchta arrived assisted by her gathering of unbaptized children, she told one of them to block the small hole in the stove door. As a result the small boy the stove managed to see nothing the whole time, and had to wait for Perchta to leave before leaving the stove himself, disappointed at not having seen anything. However when he crept out of the dark stove he realised he was now blind, unable to see a thing! As the year passed, the farmhand unable to see, he came across a hermit who advised the boy that if he went back to the stove again on the 6th of January, and did not try and spy on Perchta his eyesight might be returned. So as twelfth night approached again and the house was prepared for Perchta's visit, the boy crept back into the stove but turned away from the hole. From there he heard Perchta command the same child as before to remove the block in the hole. The boy inside the stove did not try and peak through the hole but waited for Perchta to leave again. When she did leave, he crept back out of the stove and found he was able to see again. Never again did he attempt to spy on Perchta when she returned to the farm.

The kindly cottager

The story of the cottager is a chance for the reader to see the other side of Perchta and her more benevolent side, showing us how she also has the power to reward as well as punish; a facet which is sometimes lost in retelling her tale. Following the birth of his new-born child, a humble cottager who was already struggling to feed his large family, went out into the wintery night, the snow blowing cold on his face. He had decided to set out in such a foul night to try and find a godfather for his new baby, someone who might be able to provide an improved life for the child as the cottage really had little to offer his baby apart from love. Through the blizzard and snow, he made out Perchta and her band of children coming towards him. As the children went past him, the littlest child at the back was fighting against the snow to keep up in nothing but a little bit of clothing, not enough to stop him from getting cold.

'You poor little Zodwascher!' said the cottager to the child, worried for the child's well-being in the snow. As he did Perchta wheeled around and came back towards the cottage, scaring the man.

'Since you have given the lowliest child a name, much good fortune will be yours' Perchta said to the man, before she turned and went off into the snowstorm until the cottager could not see her or any of the children. Then soon after she had gone, a man approached the villager and took him in, befriended him, and happily agreed to be his new-born baby's godfather. The man was of great wealth and provided for the cottager, his new-born, and the whole family for the rest of their lives.

The Carriage

The interesting aspect of the story of the kindly cottager is that despite her granting a blessing, the cottager is still fearful of Perchta, so admiration of her powers is also transcended into fear. This notion is also present in this next story of the carriage; again we see Perchta grant a blessing but the central character still acts under the auspice of fear throughout the story. Perchta's had travelled across the lands and through the snow as she moved from village to village across the mountains with her train of ghostly children who had died unbaptised. Approaching her next village, the road was uneven, and her carriage after such a long journey finally gave way and a wheel came off, stranding Perchta still.

Seeing the commotion from a distance, a farmhand ran to help, not knowing until he was close that it was Perchta who had lost a wheel from her carriage. Frau Perchta beckoned the farmhand over and asked him to help repair her broken carriage. The boy was afraid of Perchta but before long he realised that it was simply the linchpin from the wheel which had broken, so he took a piece of wood and carved a brand new linchpin which he placed into the wheel and repaired the carriage. Happy to have helped Perchta and to have not disappointed her, he told her his job was done. Perchta told him to keep the wooden shavings which had fallen from the block of wood he carved into the new linchpin. Too afraid to refuse, he collected the shaven wood, confused as to why he was collecting the wood he had discarded. Perchta left and the farmhand was happy to have survived. Hurrying back to his home, he emptied his pockets, planning to get rid of the wood shavings that Perchta had made him take, to his amazement when he took them from his pocket; each shaving was now made of gold.

The Twelve Spinners

No retelling of the tales of Perchta would be complete without a reference to her relationship with spinning, something with which she is frequently referenced. This tale also demonstrates a more mischievous side to Perchta; as we will come onto later, sometimes she is depicted more as a mischievous hag than an almighty beast. In the town of Ronchi, which is located in southern Tyrol, twelve women were together busily spinning away working together into the wintry night. There came a knock at the door and one of the women went to answer the door and when she opened it, there stood Frau Perchta.

She alerted the other women to her presence by saying aloud, 'good evening Frau Perchta with the long nose'.

Perchta then responded, 'Behind me is the one with a still longer nose.' She stepped inside the home, and another identical Frau Perchta was stood behind her with an even longer nose, she then stepped inside and another Perchta with an even longer nose was stood behind her. This continued until twelve Perchta's have entered the room where the women had been spinning. The twelve Frau Perchtas sat in the chairs by the spinning wheels which the women had been using.

'Bring us buckets so we can fill them with water' demanded the Perchtas. The women quickly realised what the Perchtas were wanting to do and left quickly instead bringing them baskets which could not carry water as they realised that the Perchtas were wanting to trick them into bringing water so the women could all be boiled alive. Upon given the Perchtas their baskets, they all quickly ran home to the beds to sleep.

Whilst this seems like a somewhat illogical conclusion for the women to reach regarding the threat of being boiled alive, this to any keen spinner would have been relatively clear. As one of the tasks of a spinner, they must boil their skeins, and anyone who is familiar with tasks associated with spinning may have quickly recognised that the punishment for spinning on the wrong day was the punishment involving being boiled alive. The moral is that if you spin outside of permitted times or during Perchta's festival day then a punishment would be set to match, and in this case it drew a fitting punishment which was associated to the 'crime' being committed.

The Belly-Slitter

The most infamous of tales related to that of Perchta is of her gastronomic proclivities; she is quite often merely referred to as the 'belly-slitter' and the gruesomeness of her punishment in this case is probably why she has endured as an evil legend. Perchta above all else dislikes lazy and untidy people, especially those who go to bed on her festival day of Epiphany leaving their houses in a mess. For those people who maybe leave their Christmas decorations up too long, and leave their festive food strewn across the kitchen should beware. As you and your family sleep soundly in your beds, Perchta will arrive in your room in the cold snowy night, magically like her festive cousin Santa Claus and creep over to your bed. With her tool of choice, this can be a knife, scissors, or any sharp implement, she will cut open your stomach, remove your insides, and then fill them with dirt, dust, splinters, glass, refuse, and maybe whatever things you left out in a mess around the house. She then sews your stomach back together, in some legends using the iron nose she is said to have, and then she leaves again magically. The next morning, your family awaken to find your dead body, with no signs of damage and presume you have died a natural death in the night.

This story is the most familiar amongst those who have heard the Perchta legend, her reputation for punishment rather than power to grant blessings as well as punishments is probably overshadowed by the macabre way she punishes the lazy and untidy in this story. Similar to the story above of the spinners and the fitting punishment for the crime, the filling of the body with dirt and dust for those who have not cleaned their homes shows the ingenuity of the Perchta legends to tap into appropriate threats to obtain a level of social control. A similar threat which Perchta is supposed to have undertaken is that if children lie frequently, Perchta would scrape their tongues with glass as a punishment, which again highlights how Perchta was often used as a bogeyman like character to ensure people behaved in a manner which was deemed appropriate. Perhaps the most enjoyable or frightening aspect of this last story is how closely it mirrors the Santa Claus legend, the magical visit in the night, the festive figure appearing in the bedroom whilst everybody is asleep. Yet whilst Santa is dealing with those being nice, those on the naughty list should definitely listen out for any bumps in the night around Christmas.

Appearance

As with any legend as stories are passed down generations or via word of mouth to other people, details appropriate to certain areas are added or discarded, as a result Perchta's appearance varies quite considerably. In some versions she is a beast very similar to Krampus, whilst others describe Perchta as a woman, young and old in some tales, clad in white robes which are quite contrasting. She is also described in some regions as having two faces, one on either side of her head, which is suggested reflects her dual personalities of malevolence and blessing. It may be conceivable that the Krampus like appearance that is sometimes attributed to Perchta is an amalgamation of similar Christmas creatures or that were the appearance given to her evil second face, which then became a single face as the tale was passed on.

The Krampus styled version of Perchta was similar in style to her cousin Krampus, often seen with hooves and covered in a fur, sometimes with horns. The celebrations of Perchta which we will cover later often have people who dress as Perchta dressed in masks and styles akin to this beast like Perchta. Sometimes her depiction is a combination of the two styles; both portrayed with horns, shaggy fur, and hooves of a goat but then veiled or with white garments strewn over her furry body. The hooves are a reference to her ability to shape-shift as she is sometimes attributed an ability to change into a goat when she wishes.

Sometimes Perchta's appearance is dependent on how you perceived her and whether you had done enough to please her. As we have mentioned, Perchta also had the ability to grant blessings and good tidings so her appearance was appropriate to which action she was performing. Similar to the two-faced description of Perchta, this version could appear in either incantation; either as a divine beauty clad in white robes for those who had been obedient, observed her demands, and provided the necessary foods for her on Epiphany, or as a demonic beast, horned with hooves and with a bloodlust and desire to cut open stomachs if you angered her. In the version of Perchta with two faces, these faces were both on the same head but depending on your circumstances, the good or evil face would be the one with which you were faced. Some modern day masks for Perchta celebrations have both faces on the mask which can be turned around in the same manner which the legend would be seen. Artwork often depicts Perchta with the two faces which is an artistic way of demonstrating her ability to be both kind and loving but also evil. It could conceivably be this attempt at an artistic rendition of representing her two opposing personalities which actually gave rise to the idea that she had two literal faces.

Even her human form seems to be varied depending on location of the retelling of the tale. Sometimes this was an extension of the two formed Perchta, with the good Perchta appearing beautiful and as white as snow, and the evil form as an extremely ugly, haggard woman, or sometimes just very elderly. In areas where she did not have two forms, she appeared as either version of Perchta; the beautiful Perchta both granting blessing and performing punishments. Whereas in locations such as Tyrol she is also seen as a small elderly woman with heavily wrinkled face, a long hooked nose, dishevelled straw like hair, and tattered white clothing. This version of the old Perchta is often depicted as mischievous and with the ability to trick potential victims into being punished. Her long hooked nose is another feature which transcends many version of Perchta, sometimes the beast like Perchta still has a long hooked nose, and some description suggest that the nose is actually strong as iron. There is considerable variation of the appearance of Perchta, potentially due to the passing of the legend by word of mouth but also maybe represents the being which would be most terrifying depending on the regions customs and traditions.

Another striking aspect of her appearance which is frequently referred to in many depictions of her appearance is Perchta's one oversized foot. The foot has been symbolised to mean a number of things but it also had a purpose. Another one of Perchta's ever increasing arsenal of threats was that she would use this oversized foot to crush children if they misbehaved which is potentially where the description of a large foot first arose in reference to her ability to crush children with her foot. As a result this took on other connotations as her foot was often described as similar to a goose or swan foot, which led some believers to suggest that Perchta could shape shift to an animal form if she so desired. Another suggestion as to why she has the large foot is the suggestion that the foot is a reference to her relationship with spinning. Spinners would constantly have a foot upon a treadle which turned the spinning wheel so the first references to her extra-large foot may have at first been a reference to the splayfoot of a spinner. References to her extra-large foot were frequently common in regaling the legend and references to her foot have been found in German, French, and Latin versions of the tale.

Perchta and appearance have the uncanny ability to shift into whichever form strikes the appropriate fear into a certain location or change depending on whether you see her as benevolent or malevolent. Whereas the beast form of Perchta appears popular in modern retelling of the tale, it appears to have borrowed much from other Festive monsters such as Krampus, I personally find the description which depicts her with two faces the most appropriate as it demonstrates both sides of her personality. Despite Perchta often being described as a monster of Christmas, she also had the ability to bless people for the year to come, so an appearance which reflects this delicate balance between good and evil seems most applicable to her legend.

Perchta and Food

As the reader may have noticed from reading this far, Frau Perchta and her legend has a strong affiliation with food, related to both her rewards and punishments. Whereas feasting on a hearty festive meal appears one of the best ways to fight off her belly splitting; in fact her implement for belly slitting couldn't actually pierce a stomach which was too full and also had trouble with the belly of someone who had consumed sumptuous amounts of greasy food, as the belly was thus too slippery with grease, she could sometimes also be particularly with the certain foods to be consumed on her chosen day.

The encouragement to feast or fast through traditions or superstitious customs is not limited to Perchta. You can look at Pancake Day on Shrove Tuesday for the most contemporary example of this custom. The English saying 'he who eats goose on

Michaelmas day, will never lack money his debts to pay' also alludes to the premise that gorging on a certain day has its benefits. The festive tradition of eating a mince pie each day between Christmas Day and the 6th of January is said to ensure a happy month for each mince pie consumed for the year ahead. As with nearly every aspect of the Perchta legend, there are variations in the food to be consumed. Also similar to the Santa Claus tradition, some families were encouraged to leave certain foods for Perchta to eat upon her arrival and in differing locations according to the location's traditions.

The unfortunate locals who lived in an area where the fasting was encouraged by the Perchta story were expected to eat only fish and gruel in a mark of respect to her festival day, failing to do so resulted in her customary punishment of disembowelment and taxidermy thereafter. The fasting ritual was described by Jacob Grimm but there are other traditions which enjoy the complete opposite and encouraged to gorge as much they can, as their rotund stomachs were thus too large for Perchta's knife to pierce.

For those who got to enjoy a feast to keep Perchta from slitting their bellies, they were to enjoy fried dumplings, cakes, herring, eggs, perchtenmilch or Bachlkoch, which was a traditional milk drink especially for the occasion, a porridge drizzled with honey. Some of this food was to be left for Perchta and her 'children' so milk and dumplings were often left out on a Perchtentisch (Perchta table), sometimes outside, or sometimes on the roof of a building. Sometimes this left over food was fed to farm animals as a blessing for the animals. Indeed nobody was spared from the consumption, masters and servants of the household alike were encouraged to gorge on the food to ensure a blessing was received from Perchta.

Perchta and her legend were ever evolving and synchronic to what was of importance in the age. Ensuring people feasted or fasted on certain days of the year varied in importance where Perchta was prevalent so again she was used as a social control mechanism to ensure that members of a household undertook certain dietary behaviours. Whereas her rewards were less commonly referenced, using her punishments were a convenient way of ensuring certain behaviours were met, in the case of food, fast or feast on appropriate days of the year. It was certainly a threat which was directed at the young in the house; which maybe highlights how Perchta was used to maybe encourage behavioural control of children. The below rhyme which was attributed to Perchta highlighted that children were often the target of her benevolence.

Kinder oder Speck,

Darweil geheich nicht weg!

Children or bacon,

Or I won't go away!

The rhyme has been attributed to other witches in folklore, including Baba Raga in Russia, but again demonstrates that the punishment of poor behaviour was recanted with more frequency that the rewards and blessings that Perchta was said to grant.

In case any reader wishes to have a go at appeasing the legend of Perchta, or maybe receive a blessing for the year ahead, below is the recipe for Bachlkoch, the traditional milky porridge which was said to please our legend when prepared and eaten on her festival day. However it comes with a warning as it is said not to be the most straight forward recipe and none of us want an angered Perchta and her minions visiting us on the 12th night this year.

Bachlkoch

500ml of Milk

40g of white flour

Pinch of salt

2 tablespoons of butter

2 tablespoons of honey

Method:

-Bring the milk to a gentle boil in a pan, slowly whisking and ensuring that the milk does not burn or overflow.

-The tricky part is next which could be aided by having a handy assistant. Whilst stirring the milk, use a sieve to gently add the flour to the milk, letting the flour 'snow' into the mixture. Try to avoid lumps of flour in the milk as Frau Perchta can be easily riled by flour lumps.

-Continue to stir until the milk and flour become creamy in texture and then remove from the heat.

-Add the pinch of salt and stir in the butter. Stir the ingredients until the butter melts and ensure that the Bachlkoch does not have a layer of skin, this is another dislike of Perchta.

-Finally to serve add some honey, drizzling it across the Bachlkoch and enjoy!

As with many recipes, this can vary from household to household, but generally something sweet is added as a final touch, honey the most common addition. Sometimes a sprinkle of oatmeal is added to make the food a little more filling. The Bachlkoch recipe is notoriously difficult to obtain as there are so many variations and there is little divulgence in how to make the perfect Bachlkoch, even the internet provides little information. This could well be because traditional Bachlkoch is dying away with older generations, but you never know, maybe those who have been making perfect Bachlkoch through the ages have been pleasing Frau Perchta year on year and do not want to share their blessings! Have a go at the recipe, but beware, Frau Perchta is very particularly about the recipe only being prepared on her festival day, 6th of January.

Perchta in history

For many readers of this book, Perchta may have been an unknown festive entity but has she always been this way? Hidden away in the alpine regions in small villages? The answer is no if you include all the different interpretations of her legend; she may have gone by a different name but the Christmas belly-slitter was alive and well across many European regions. She was present across much of Germany, France, Switzerland, Austria, Slovenia, and popped up in other countries sporadically. The name Perchta which this book has chosen as it is her most recognisable name perhaps hides how widespread she was because Perchta was known under many pseudonyms. To list a few to exemplify how far reaching her legend really was; Perahta, Berchte, Behrta, Frau Faste, Pehta, Kvaterniam, Posterli, Quatemberca, Fronfastenweiber, Berigl, Berchtlmuada, Perhta-Baba, Zlobna, Sampa, Stampa, Lutzl, Zamperin, Pudelfrau, Bechtrababa, Zampermuatta. Now, I wouldn't suggest you recognise any of these names but for one legend to have so many names and interpretations perhaps demonstrates how far her story was told across Europe in her heyday.

The actual name of Perchta is said to derive from the Old High German language for 'the bright one' which was the word *beraht,* the word also highlights her link to the epiphany as Berchta which she is frequently referenced as, comes from the word *Berchtentag* which can be taken to mean 'the feast of epiphany'. But how did our festive maiden impact upon those who lived under the auspice of her legend when it was at the height of its popularity? Well she definitely was a big enough of a phenomenon for her to cause the Christian church enough of a headache for them to increasingly portray Perchta as an evil beast rather than the dual natured legend she was frequently described as, she shown by the stories provided earlier. Pagan religions, of which Perchta (as many of our festive deities are related), is closely aligned, have an alternate view of good and evil from what some modern religions are more accustomed. Deities such as Perchta were revered for their almighty power rather than for being a benevolent being. As we have seen Perchta could indeed be rewarding and bless her followers but in general for her followers, a level of obedience to the most powerful incantation of a god came before the importance of any social goods. This contrasted with the views of Christianity as it sought to become the religion of the masses; God for Christianity was a force for good and a provider of morals for their followers. This caveat coupled with the fact that there was no space for other deities such as Perchta meant that the Church sought to remove Perchta's omniscience power. Christianity however knew that they would not be able to eradicate Perchta so quickly as she had become ingrained into local customs and traditions, especially during winter, so they moved to play down the aspects of her character which may have challenged God's almighty good. They encouraged the tales which foretold her evil ways and her punishments and downplayed the stories of her blessings; it may have been from this religious manoeuvring that Perchta is still considered with such fear as a ghoul of Christmas. We do have records from the Christian Church of 'sinners' who continued to revere in Perchta's power during Medieval periods; this was often demonstrated, much to the chagrin of the Church, by believers who continued to leave food for Perchta on Twelfth Night in return for prosperity in the coming year. There are other records that despite the commands of the Church many regions continued to offer their prayers to 'Frawen Percht' before the Virgin Mary. Whilst the strategy of Christianity did prevail against the Pagan characters such as Perchta, she potentially managed to stay so ingrained due the flexibility of the tales told about her; she managed to remain prevalent and contemporary due to the ability of her tales to incorporate topics of the era.

Spinning, with which she is so closely related in many tales, was of prevalence in the era when Perchta was at the height of her popularity and could in part explain her ongoing survival before losing her importance as spinning was to also lose importance to family life. Many Perchta tales revolved around spinning, and she generally can be seen now in hindsight as a method of social control, both ensuring that spinning was not done on days of relevance (i.e. Twelfth Night) or that spinning duties were not neglected during the year as she punished both those who failed to complete a set amount of work, and those who performed spinning on forbidden days of the year. Both 'crimes' could be met with the usual punishments, bad luck for the year ahead or the more severe belly slitting. This level of influence was measured out down to the levels of spinning which included shepherds. They too were said to regularly see Perchta in the mountains and hills where they kept their livestock, walking in the summer with a golden spindle in her hand. She was central to the completion on a season's spinning targets and ensured that everyone met their quotas with the fear of her legend hanging over their activities. This relationship to spinning maintained her importance for as long as spinning remained an important activity to households and ensured her legend was passed on, warning future spinners not to be idle with their work for the fear of Perchta's night time visit to remove your entrails.

However as with many a legend, it can be festivities which prolong their longevity. If you look to Bonfire Night in the UK as an example of how Guy Fawkes and the gunpowder plot has been remembered continuously for over 400 years; our ability to pass on stories is greatly aided by celebrations. The legend of Perchta has no doubt continued to this day, albeit in pockets of locations, due to the celebrations in these areas which regale the story of Perchta. However whereas these were not celebrations keeping the story alive, which we will come to, originally, the celebrations were part of the belief in Perchta's omniscient power and presence.

The Perchtenlauf was the most popular of rituals across regions which celebrated Perchta's presence, and generally involved a procession of men dressed in costumes with masks which were decorated to look like the venerated fearsome Perchta. The celebration was festive and merry but it also had a purpose and was more akin to a ritual than an all celebration as it is nowadays. The men dressed in their masks would move from house to house in their village and their fearful masks would scare away the evil spirits which inhabited the winter season. Generally this was performed on Winter Solstice as this is the longest night of the year so for the villagers of the era, the peak night of winter. This is also an example of how Perchta really is a festive witch, her influence from Solstice through to Twelfth Night. The villagers knew that after solstice, the spring would soon be on the way, and Perchta was summoned via this ritual to frighten away the winter season, and bring on the warmth of the spring season. Whereas this ritual may seem nothing more than a reason for locals to dress up and chase around the village house to house, during this period, hundreds of years ago, the winter months did bring on months of cold and difficulty which for some villagers would have been fatal. The festivities were also a way for the village to rally together and bring hope for the oncoming season; it could be surmised that it was this hope in the ritual which eventually transformed it into the modern jovial celebration.

Perchtenlaufen was not the only ritual which was performed; other similar rituals took place, but usually with an emphasis on scaring away Perchta, which different from Perchtenlaufen which summoned Perchta to scare away spirits. In Austria's *Wilde Jagd* folklore festivity, the similar use of men dressed in masks occurred, but they then went around the village with sticks and clubs in a frenzy of noises and frivolity in chasing Perchta away from the village. The actual ritual was similar in nature, but Perchta in this rendition is not summoned, she is frightened away by the fearsome masks. These Austrian festivities were accompanied by burning of special herbs and smoking of the homes in the village. This tradition was thought to awaken the good spirits related to spring and the coming of the New Year from their slumber beneath winter's snow. Similar celebrations across regions where Perchta was popular took place during the festive period; much like her legend and dual roles, these celebrations either took to summoning Perchta to bring the village luck or sought to banish the witch from visiting the village. Whatever the custom, the Perchtenlaufen celebrations were both a ritual to bring about fortune for the village but also a celebration of noises and dance and creativity; a tradition which has continued through to present day.

Modern celebrations

That the annual festive celebrations of Perchtenlauf have continued to this day from their medieval beginnings is an incredible feat and they have continued to grow in popularity, now becoming a tourist attraction in some of the Alps based ski resorts that have adopted the celebrations. The increase in popularity in contemporary culture has kept Perchta's legend continuing and she is still seen as rewarding the generous and punishing the bad, a true festive spirit. Places such as Salzberg have embraced the traditional Perchtenlaufen celebrations, the traditional carving of fearsome masks have become a showcase in themselves, masks now rival each other for authenticity, fear factors, and elaborate headpieces.

An intriguing facet of the modern day celebration is the festivities flamboyant depiction of Perchta's kind and evil sides, which draws together many aspects of the older celebrations into a frenzied like atmosphere. Each celebration has its own traditions and customs relevant to the location, the most famous Perchtenlaufen in Salzberg is celebrated on every Thursday on the 3 weeks prior to Christmas. The *Perchten*, the name given to those who disguise themselves in costumes, appear in double form. One set, the *Schönpechten* (the beautiful perchten), who are handsomely clad in traditional costume of the regions. The beautiful perchten are bright and beautifully dressed and are supposed to encourage economic prosperity for the village, bringing luck and wealth as they dance around in procession. The Schiachperchten (the ugly perchten) represent the dark side of Perchta, their faces hidden behind terrifying wooden carved masks, usually clothes in fur and black garments. They too run around, with bells from their costumes jingling and the sound of whips and ecstatic screeches as they add to the frivolity of the festivities. These large processions of the ugly perchten are said to drive away the evil spirits, which draws from the traditional Perchtenlaufen festivals. The Schiachperchten with their fangs, tusks, and horned masks go from house to house to drive away any evil winter spirits who may be hiding. The end result of the procession is an array of sound, sights, and action, the two sides of Perchta represented artistically through movement, costume, and dance. Other festivals, the *Tresterer, Schnabelpercht,* and *Glöcklerlaufen* all display the same joyful frenzy and atmosphere, with bells, masks, characters on stilts, all portraying their regions depiction of Perchta.

It is a joy to see how Perchta and her legend has had a renaissance in contemporary festive celebrations, the festivals now draw thousands of tourists to numerous processions in different locations across Europe. The creative masks and costumes have taken on a life of their own, but many of the locals have begun to again warn of Frau Perchta wandering through winter the Austrian hills, so maybe her legend is rekindling as more and more people again start to witness the procession of the Festive belly-slitter.

Conclusion

During the 20th century, Christmas ghouls and anti-Santas appeared to lose their importance as festive figures, as Father Christmas boomed in popularity but over the last decade or so, these fearsome festive creatures have had a small renaissance, led mainly be the increased popularity of Krampus. As the media consume the legends with new books, music, and films inspired by the legends of terrifying Christmas monsters, older legends have also rekindled. Perchta's festivals which have continued since medieval times have now become a tourist attraction and a mainstay of the festive calendar for some Alpine ski resorts and draw ever increasing crowds. Threatening figures and boogeymen have died out in the modern day lexicon, Christmas for contemporary children offers rewards or the threat of receiving nothing; long gone are the threats of a beating from a Christmas ghoul, let alone a disembowelment made popular by Perchta. Figures such as Perchta should be considered within their context, looking at her legend and her role through the eras, the diachronic perspective showed how she adapted to stay relevant. Maybe there is no context for her currently to be utilised as a Christmas ogre; our food consumption is not as vital as it once was, spinning is now long relevant to modern era, and conceptions of laziness are altering with the advent of technology. Frau Perchta has always been the enforcer of communal taboos, rewarding and punishing as deemed appropriate, she survives due to her incarnation's flexibility to the taboos of new eras. All it takes is for the legend to be appropriated to a new form of social control; too much internet, too much TV, or too much Xbox. Frau Perchta continues to survive as long as people continue to adapt her as a threatening figure, making her applicable to present day contexts. Hopefully this book has passed on her legend and given the reader enough information that they too can wield the power of Perchta's legend. Next time you leave a mince pie and brandy out on Christmas Eve, just have an extra think to who you are dedicating those Christmas treats.

Word from the Author

Thank you for reading Frau Perchta: A concise history, I do hope you enjoyed reading about the legend. I love the festive season and I find the different legends of good and evil captivating, they are wonderful reads for beside a cosy Christmas fire. There are some incredible books available on the history of many of the legends but I felt like Frau Perchta had been neglected to an extent hence writing this book.

If you have any feedback on the book or just want to say hello, you can find me on twitter @EdBreckin and I will always be happy to answer any questions to the best of my knowledge.

Please leave a review on amazon, whether it is positive or negative as the feedback can help me in writing other books in the 'Concise History' series. I also welcome suggestions for other supernatural themed books which I can look into covering in the future.

Thanks again for reading and please do say hello on twitter.

Merry Christmas!

Ed Breckin

Made in United States
North Haven, CT
21 December 2023

46386888R00039